Written by S.A. Brathwaite
Illustrations by Rodney Sanon

First Edition
ISBN paper 978-0-5788-9220-7
ISBN digital 978-0-5788-9221-4

Library of Congress Cataloging-in-Publication Data

To UAB, my brilliant, beautiful, encouraging, and funny partner. I see you and appreciate all you do.

To AAB and MAB, I love you more than life itself. Don't take any of this personally... well, maybe just a bit of it.

This is my family.

Me, my mom, my dad, my little brother,
and our dog, Buster.

Before my baby brother was born, Mom used to work
all day at her job.

But now she doesn't have to do any work!

Mom gets to stay home with me and my brother because he's just a baby.

I think Mom really just wants to stay home so she can play with me... but she doesn't want to admit it.

Mom says her home job is harder than her regular job.

I don't have any money, so I give her lots of hugs and kisses.

Mom says she can't wait until
after bedtime so she can have
some of her Special Juice.

Sometimes Mom needs a break, so I try to play quietly.

But when I am quiet for too long she comes looking for me.

I made an art project in the bathroom. Mom liked it so much,
we went right back to the store to get more art supplies.

And Special Juice for later.

Mom took us to the playground so I could run around.

She said she didn't feel like giving me a bath so I should NOT head straight for the sandbox.

I always listen to my mom.
I played in the sprinklers first.

Mom said once she puts us to bed, she is *definitely* having some Special Juice.

Dad came home early.
He surprised Mom.

She was so happy her
face turned red.

And then we had pizza for dinner. **Hooray!!**

After dinner, Mom said I had thirty minutes
to get my last bit of energy out before a bath
and bedtime.

I decided to play fetch outside with Buster.

Mom thinks I don't know about Buster's fetch stick,

but I know where she hides it.

Mom said she needed a break, so Dad gave me a bath tonight.
He said he hoped I didn't give Mom a hard time today.

I told him, "I was no trouble at all!"

Mom came back to tuck me into bed and read me a story.
Mom said that it's days like today that she misses her job.

I love my mom. She never gets tired or sleepy.
I want to be just like her when I grow up.

Mom said she was finally going to have her Special Juice once I went to sleep.

Mom and Dad gave me kisses and wished me good night.

But I can't sleep.

I wonder what Mom is doing.

Mom's Special Juice tastes bad!

"Mom! I think your juice is spoiled!"

THE
END

CPSIA information can be obtained
at www.ICGtesting.com
Printed in the USA
BVHW011928041121
620792BV00003BA/74

Written by S.A. Brathwaite
Illustrations by Rodney Sanon

First Edition
ISBN paper 978-0-5788-9220-7
ISBN digital 978-0-5788-9221-4

Library of Congress Cataloging-in-Publication Data

To UAB, my brilliant, beautiful, encouraging, and funny partner. I see you and appreciate all you do.

To AAB and MAB, I love you more than life itself. Don't take any of this personally... well, maybe just a bit of it.

This is my family.

Me, my mom, my dad, my little brother,
and our dog, Buster.

Before my baby brother was born, Mom used to work
all day at her job.

But now she doesn't have to do any work!

Mom gets to stay home with me and my brother because he's just a baby.

I think Mom really just wants to stay home so she can play with me... but she doesn't want to admit it.

Mom says her home job is harder than her regular job.

I don't have any money, so I give her lots of hugs and kisses.

Mom says she can't wait until
after bedtime so she can have
some of her Special Juice.

Sometimes Mom needs a break, so I try to play quietly.

But when I am quiet for too long she comes looking for me.

I made an art project in the bathroom. Mom liked it so much,
we went right back to the store to get more art supplies.

And Special Juice for later.

Mom took us to the playground so I could run around.

She said she didn't feel like giving me a bath so I should NOT head straight for the sandbox.

I always listen to my mom.
I played in the sprinklers first.

Mom said once she puts us to bed, she is *definitely* having some Special Juice.

Dad came home early.
He surprised Mom.

She was so happy her
face turned red.

And then we had pizza for dinner. **Hooray!!**

After dinner, Mom said I had thirty minutes
to get my last bit of energy out before a bath
and bedtime.

I decided to play fetch outside with Buster.

Mom thinks I don't know about Buster's fetch stick,

but I know where she hides it.

Mom said she needed a break, so Dad gave me a bath tonight.
He said he hoped I didn't give Mom a hard time today.

I told him, "I was no trouble at all!"

Mom came back to tuck me into bed and read me a story.
Mom said that it's days like today that she misses her job.

I love my mom. She never gets tired or sleepy.
I want to be just like her when I grow up.

Mom said she was finally going to have her Special Juice once I went to sleep.

Mom and Dad gave me kisses and wished me good night.

But I can't sleep.

I wonder what Mom is doing.

Mom's Special Juice tastes bad!

"Mom! I think your juice is spoiled!"

THE
END

CPSIA information can be obtained
at www.ICGtesting.com
Printed in the USA
BVHW011928041121
620792BV00003BA/74